UNDER THE COVER

PAPER & FABRIC BOOKS

FRANCES PICKERING

I dedicate this book
to my dear friend
Lindsay Jane Griffiths

In my experience of teaching, the main problem people have is how to fill the books they have made — in this book I have endeavoured to offer some inspiration and help towards filling.

In addition to making books using paper, fabric can be used successfully for covers and pages resulting in rich textured books.

'Under the Cover' of this book hopefully you will find help to get started ....

M.Pickering 2012....

This entire book has
all been drawn, written
and stitched on fabric
– everything is actual
size to the original.

3.

FULL OF IDEAS

1930's/40's Needlework

flowers

30s fabric?

Embroidery and Needlework 1945.

flower drawn from [...] on fabric – table [...] coloured with waters[...] Ink Blocks ....

'Stitches are a means to an end in needlework not an end themselves. They are the words of our needle language; without them we cannot speak'......

1940s transfer ironed onto old sheet – used as background – vintage threads.

Keep a book to put your ideas in – even things you might have written on scraps of paper. Make your own ideas book – from fabric or an assortment of papers.......

An ideas book doesn't have to be a sketchbook! Stick stitch or pin things in .... a reference book for the future ......

Stitches used.
chain
double-chain
zig-zag chain
interlaced chain
whipped chain.

flowers drawn from 1930 embroidery transfer onto a cotton sheeting...

coloured pencil.

open chain...

chain stitch used a lot on tray cloth and chair covers.

patterns from transfers.

feathered chain....

5.

m at

as and

out

dow

front

- Gesso

d?

ic

s or

?

ls

?

e

Derwent
Colowsoft

und Derwent
Graphtint

...ded
_...h_
and
...paint
method
for
...ses

→ bonded onto background and mach
and hand stitched.

Primroses fr...
child of
Merry Spr...
ha...
With her...

"Live, primrose, then, and thrive

With thy true number five;

John Donne .....

Shakeop...

2 layers of tissue bonded together.

An ideas book can be made from anything......
brown paper, wrapping paper, carrier bags.
Whatever you have to hand......

baking parchment
watersolub[...]
ink blocks

acrylic wax

watersoluble ink blocks —
wonderful for blending. Can
be used on fabric or all
sorts of paper.

ink blocks applied to
wet sponge and pinned
when dry — translucent
little effect — permanent.

Use the book to try out new materials......

thin card......

watersoluble ink blocks

...... paper and lace

drawn on fabric with candle, first - then ink blocks - didn't work.

A cover can be made from paper and fabric......

If you have nothing else use string..........
to hold it together.....

...fabric flowers....

9.

Leaves

Oak
Aspen.
Norway Maple
Sweet
Chesnot.
Spindle.
Lime.
Wild Cherry
Birch.
Hawthorn
Poplar

Leaf drawn
on cotton sheet
coloured with
tea —
coloured
with
ink blocks......

charles
Dickens.

Autumn leaves, autumn
leaves

lie strewn
are me
here;

Withered leaves,
withered leaves
Ye tell a mournful
tale........

Pages of pages cut
to leaf shape

Gesso painted
on old
printed
into
when
wet.......
tablecloth...

10.

small idea books
can still contain lots
of experiments.....

two layers of abaca tissue...

autumn...

leaves —

g colour.

shapes.

veins make
printing
block

printed onto cotton.

drawn onto with pencil.

leaf rubbed over
with wax
crayon...

As leaves dry out they
become
translucent

leaves cut out of goosebree fabric

baking parchment
painted with
acrylic paint

colour pages and tear them before
you begin... this makes the book
less intimidating!.....

COVERS.

The cover of the book is critical. It is the first thing you see and leads you into the inside. It needs to be durable. Try experimenting with different materials.

2.

3.

12.

Remember to think about fastenings when planning your cover. It could be an important part of your design.

Always apply acrylic wax to your cover BEFORE stitching. One to three coats applied thinly is enough.

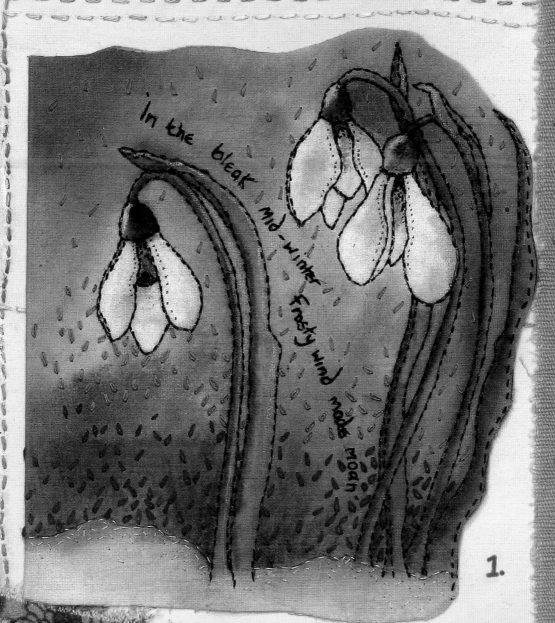

In the bleak mid-winter frosty wind made moan

1.

1. Above book... painted calico. A thin layer of acrylic wax was then applied.
2. A thin layer of Gesso was applied to calico, painted then acrylic wax applied. Leaf cut out of same fabric.
3. Printed and dyed fabrics have been combined to create a soft fabric cover.

14.

Fabulous t...
desires   Vita Sackvi... West

15.

That virgin, vital,
beautiful day,
today

A pocket on the front of a book can hold little ...

A thin layer of Gesso has been applied to brown paper which has been bonded to cotton fabric for support. Printed into when still wet....

16.

Cover ready for stitching.
Fabric paint background
on fine Calico. Overprinted
with acrylic paint. Cut to
shape, then details filled
in with black pen......

Alpaca Tissue bonded
felt. Painted with
machine stitched ink, to

17.

The world's a garden

Pleasures are the flowers

Thrice Welcome sweet summer in softness returning:

PAGES

All sorts of materials can be used for your book pages. Experimenting with different sorts of fabric and paper can produce exciting results.

calico · old cotton sheet · wallpaper lining paper · tablecloth · fine linen fabric · handkerchiefs bonded together

'Autumn leaves, autumn leaves, autumn leaves, lie strewn around me here; Autumn leaves, autumn leaves how sad, how cold, how drear!...

leaves, how sad, how cold, how drear...

Old cotton sheet painted with watered down gesso. Leaf has been painted and stitched to edge of page and then bonded to show page underneath... and bonded to show back page cut back

20.

Bonded sheet.. painted and stitched. bonded to page.

....old sheet painted and drawn into....

Edge away...→

There are always flowers for those who want to see them. Matisse.

sheets of brown paper bonded together. pale printed cotton.

I find I get the best results by bonding the thinner fabrics together.

Fine Muslin.....

old sheet painted with watered down gesso.....

Table cloth....

light weight calico....

old cotton sheet.....

Fine linen fabric.....

Abaca Tissue...

All of the above have been painted with waterbased dyes.....

21.

ASSEMBLING

Take care when you are assembling your book. do not rush the process.

Glue or bond your lining to your cover.....

Attach your fastening before making up

Rubber bands can be used.....

Large paper clips hold everything together firmly.....

Use a large needle and strong thread three times the length of the book.....

Come up here

B

A

5 Come up through top hole.

6 Go under... twist stitch

2 Go through centre...

4 Go down centre again.

1. Hold this end

7. Pull A + B tight and tie together

3

Never use bulldog clips to hold your book together they will mark your pages.

In the Celtic world it was believed that Daisies were the spirits of children who had died at birth...

FEBRUARY 13 MOON DAISY

Always make an odd number of holes.....

22.

The one delicious green that now provides...

Linings can be machine stitched or hand stitched. If you are applying acrylic wax... do it first....

Linings can be made of fabric or paper whatever is suitable...

TOO SCARED TO START?

If you don't start, how do you know what you can do? Drawing is about confidence. If you start with something simple and then branch out into more challenging subjects, you might surprise yourself.

Based on Medieval manuscripts... A border on the edge of a page writing on a page look very attractive.

Not all drawing has to be naturalistic

If you are worried about using colour .... try using black and white....

Black and White is a good starting point, add colour gradually. Remember you will be adding stitch at some point when you are making and filling your book ..... be brave and get started !!!

Add a touch of colour...

Pen drawings can look very striking...

six children... three girls three boys...

Culpeper writes '... a wound herb of good respect!'... Ox-Eye daisies can grow to a metre or more... Ox-Eye Daisy...

The leaves contain digoxin... The leaves. more so the leaves are poisonous... small doses this is used for heart medicine... Foxglove... Though the dye is red the flowers are blue...

Red Clover... The clover flower is rich in ... therefore essential for ... sometimes called ... big ball... Sometimes called or Moon Daisy... Green Alkanet ... are edible...

26.

Nor rural sights alone, but rural sounds, Exhilarate the spirit, and restore the tone of languid Nature.

Baby 6...

Monpazier is a medieval fortified 'Bastide'. Founded in 1284 by the English King - Edward I.

PORTE DU PARADIS

a doorway and window grills......

Try drawing and painting on different surfaces........

Bird drawn on Abaca Tissue......

Butterflies drawn on Gesso painted cotton sheet!....

↑ Tissue with painted acrylics.

tree drawn on a cotton sheet

All the surfaces on this page can be stitched into...

Could be a front cover?

↑ Fine linen fabric painted with acrylic and drawn onto with pencils.

Keep it simple at first..... build up your skills.
Practise makes perfect.
Don't give up!!

Start with a very simple shape......

Try adding lines and shapes......

Add a few marks...

A simple pencil drawing...

Draw on a front cover ?.....

Draw on fabric and create colour and texture with stitch ....

29.

FABRIC BOOKS

Making a fabric book can be very satisfy
There is often no need to buy any fabric
as all sorts of scraps and collected materials
that you have tucked away
can be used....

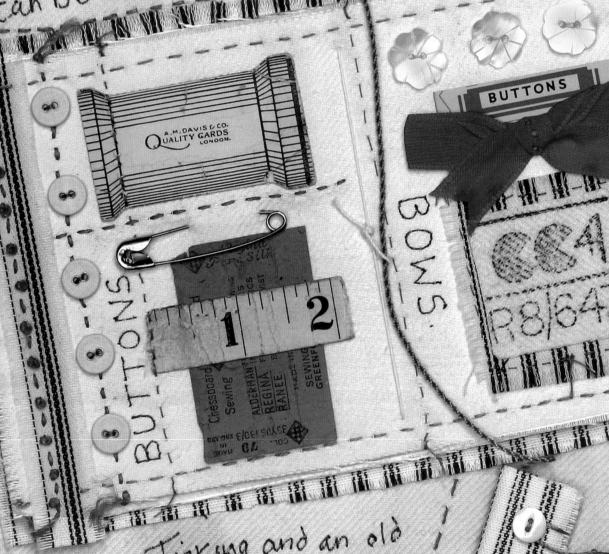

↗ Mattress Ticking and an old
Second World War sheet have
been used to make this book...

Scraps of precious fabrics can be put in your book...

Can't remember the original colour.

Overdyed it three times.

Favourite dress — wore it so often the material became very thin.

An old cotton shirt was dyed with tea and then cut up to make this book. The shirt cuff was used for the fastening...

31.

'Nature's first green
gold,
hardest hue to hold.
early leaf's a flower,
but only so an hour'.....
Robert Frost..

Then leaf subsides
to leaf'.....

Above - printed fabric can be used for
pages if plain fabric is bonded on top. The leaf
motif has been picked up from the printed
fabric.. A small fabric envelope has been added

Below - a piece of 1950s fabric has
been used, leaves in keeping with the
period have been printed onto very
fine linen. The cover has then been
machine stitched and hand stitched.

'The Butterfly upon
the sky,
That doesn't
Know its Name
And hasn't any tax to pay
And hasn't any Home
Is just as high as you and I,
And higher, I believe,
So soar away and never sigh
And that's the way to grieve'....
Emily Dickinson...

'From Cocoon forMa
Butterfly.'

The above book
was made from old
green linen. Soft
fine linen is easy
to print and write on.
Butterflies have been
printed on the pages and
then drawn into with pen
and coloured pencils. Cut outs
from magazines or photocopies
could also be used....

Now Autumn's fire burns slowly along the

And day by day the dead leaves fall and melt

William Allingham.....

...and the noise of a sea breaking on sand and stone'....

34.

'Sow Kind Acts and Memory's garden will smell sweet!....

The British needle where merchant leads..... Ann Macbeth

BEAUP

35.

SOMETHING TO SAY?

You might know exactly what you want to say. If you don't, there are many sources to help you — books, the internet, songs, folklore etc. Often words can be the inspiration for a book...........

You don't always have to just write on pages - the inside cover can be used as well.....

'I loved thee, though I told thee not

Right early and long, Thou wert my joy in every spot,

My theme in every song

John Clare.

POETRY

The whole of the book can be centred round poetry..........

← letters can be cut out of fabric

Just living is not enough, said the butterfly, 'one must have sunshine, freedom and a little flower

Come fly with me...

sometimes letters need to be very small..........

Sometimes it is easier to write on the back of printed fabric ..... the words show up clearer and are more effective.....:

Words form the thread on which we string our experiences' Aldous Huxley

The STITCH of a book is its WORDS... Rumer Godden.

Dandelion

writing on linen fabric is not easy - stitching over the words make it look neater

LAVENDER BLUE

DILLY DILLY

LAVENDER GREEN

Common flower beside the way ... to make with beauty's gay

Happiness is to hold flowers in both hands.

PILGRAMAGES

Thanne longen folk to goon on
PILGRAMAGES
And palmers for to seken straunge
strondes,
To ferne halwes, kowthe in sondry
londes;
And specially from every shires
ende.
Of engelond to caunterbury they
wende,
The hooly blisful martir for to
seke,
That hem hath holpen whan
that they were seeke.'

Busy old fool, unruly Sunne,
Why dost thou thus,
Through windows, and
through curtains
call on us? .
John
Donne.

'One cannot collect all the
beautiful
shells on the beach; one can collect
only a few, and they are more
beautiful if they are few'.
Anne Morrow Lindbergh...

38.

'I love at eventide
to walk alone
Down narrow lanes
o'erhung with
dewy thorn'.

GREATER STICHWORT

John Clare

FORGET-ME-NOT

- The trees are coming into leaf
Like something almost being said.
Philip Larkin

'The fields and
garden-borders
Are bright
because of
SPRING.

Violet Jacob.

colouring your lined paper before working on it makes it so much more interesting.....

All the elements on the page can have equal status......

There is nothing wrong with using lined paper if it makes you feel more confident make it more inter... colouring the paper will

Then followed that beautiful Summer season Longfellow...

keep a book to put all your quotes sayings and poetry in.....

'Raised are the dripping oars', Silent the boat! the lake Lovely and soft as a dream. Swims in the sheen of the moon Matthew Arnold.

I believe a leaf of grass is no less than the journey-work of the stars Walt Whitman.

'Embroidery is a very personal art, its charm lies in the individuality expressed by the worker.

W.G Paulson Townsend 1899.

'Come then, come, some quiet hour, O'er book, or needle dream. Gather here and there a flower - Find thyself in them!' Walter de la Mare.

FABRIC AND LACE FABRIC AND LACE !

Old sheets work well as pages and are easy to write on. This piece has lace underneath the fabric which has then been rubbed over with water soluble ink blocks.

When writing on paper or fabric make sure you use a waterproof pen...

Make sure your pen is waterproof on fabric as well as on paper. Wait a few minutes for the ink to dry on the fabric before ....testing it....

PROSE.

write with pencil as well as pen......

Fit words into spaces ......

DOORS AND WINDOWS EVERYWHERE......

UN REST
LAUGHTER TIMELESS
SMILES PEACE
FRIENDS SPIRITUAL
LOVE

soft pencils can be used to write with.

TAKING A WALK

There are many reasons to walk - walking the dog, children to school, around your village or town. A book could be ma[de] If you are a regular walker or rambler you can record your walks... from an [...] of thes[e]

MORE IDEAS FOR BOOKS.

Peyre marchand - France. Walked in the woods most days. Nearly in the woods were strewn with a multitude of leaves and broken.

puffball mushrooms

wild herbs
wild thyme and mi[...]

parasol mushrooms

ivy wrapped around a tree....

Joe & Zoe's Peyremarchand
walnuts fallen from the tree..

There's still some wild flowers in the woods and fields. The paths

Jays making a n[oise] in the trees up above. Try as we might we couldn't see them.

Keep walkers notebooks

You don't always have to draw writing and stitch looks great....

keep a record for later...........

Walkin Woods - 26th Oct.
with Keith and
Christine. So
many pinecones,
Keith went back
for the Car!!

↖ a very small
notebook keep in
your pocket....

chesnuts
everyshere....

medlar tree

Buzzards
flying overhead

butterflies
across the
meadow.

Malbernat.
David and Snowys →

yarrow still
in flower   and lots of
seedheads

...y was
...rled around
...he
...lectricity
...pole... Chanterelle
mushrooms

Draw or ↗
write directly
onto
fabric

walking back
home.....

France....

November.....

Brightly coloured caterpillar
it will turn into a Goat Moth....

October....
There are still a few
wild flowers about.....

A SPECIAL PLACE

A special place can be somewhere you visit often or have particularly happy memories of as a child. It could be your garden, park or even your workroom, whatever inspires you to create a book...

EVEN MORE IDEAS FOR BOOKS.....

A quick sketch can be made or take photographs or write descriptions. All can be used later....

machine stitched outline?

leaves cut out of a brochure coloured with Inktense blocks

HAWKWOOD SPRING...

It can help to sit, shut your eyes and think of a list of words that come to mind.......

photocopy a sketch and later........ add

...Twisted hedges.....Windows....sheep....peace.....bluebells.....fun......

Draw, print or photocopy...

Capture your memories in your own way – fabric, stitch, illustration, photocopy, brochures, use found objects etc...

Stitch before adding to book...

fabric or paper can be used...

...tissue bonded onto felt and stitched...

Add your own special touches...

'First, April, she with mellow showers
Opens the way for early flowers;
Then after her comes smiling May'
ROBERT HERRICK.

'Primroses first, born child of ver,
Merry Springtimes harbinger
with her bells dim!'...
SHAKESPEARE.

THURSDAY

As we drove into Hawkwood... as usual the field was full of wild flowers. Cowslips are special - standing up so proud. We saw a whole bank as we drove here... a mass of creamy yellow...

45.

THE SEASIDE

There are so many aspects of the seaside to explore.. If you don't want to print or draw, cut out pictures from magazines or brochures.....

IDEAS FOR BOOKS

Keep the background colour of the pages, pale and soft.........

....SEA — SAND — SUN — WAVES — SEAGULLS — FISH

Some pages can be cut in the shape of waves.....

Who hath desired the Sea?
- the sight of salt water unbounded -
he heave and the halt and the hurl

Gesso spread on linen drawn into..
Painted with acrylic paint whilst dry

Mould make a good cover

Fish painted with metallic acrylics....

nd crash of the comber wind-hounded......

Rudyard Kipling......

SHELLS...... ROCKPOOLS ...... SAND CASTLES ...... CRABS ...... PEBBLES..

beaded edge...

seeding......

The edge of the page can be cut to shape

seagull painted with fabric paint on fine cotton fabric

• Live in the sunshine
swim the sea...
drink the wild air. '
Ralph Waldo Emerson..

Tiny known

stitch ideas...

"My life
As near the ocean's edge as
I can go"
...Thoreau...

Ralph

...full of longing
For the secret of the sea.

And the heart of the great ocean
Sends a thrilling pulse...
Longfellow

48.

Merr

Skelton.

Thomas
Becket

Born in London in 1118

49.

DAY BY DAY.

Suitable patterned fabric also works well ... ↓

Journals and diaries can be made out of fabric or paper. Try a combination of both!

beautiful hips.

September 6th

3rd September.

walnuts an glace cherrie

Made a cof walnut cake. I am still us Mum's recipe and always put glace cherries on the

chocolate sweets...

I made chocolate cupcak ... I do love baking !!

It is not difficult to write on fabric and then add stitch.

Photocopies, recipes, photograph

18th November
Sarlat...
Visited the lovely old linen shop in Sarlat again. Came here a couple of weeks ago with Christine ... we had such a lovely time looking at all the beautiful things. Jim bought me fabric this time - such lovely old pieces!

5th September...
Daisy starts school this week, it will be Grace's second year. Becky sent me a lovely photograph...

A 'Haberdashery Journal'...

A family memory journal can hold precious memories...

etc. can be added.......

Very wild windy day didn't stay too long!!

little clumps of violets

Wonderful banks and hedgerows...

bluebells
honesty
lesser spearwort
cuckooflower
daisy

May 2012 Charing

Daisies all over the lawn. The grass has been growing like mad with all the rain. I think the daisy is my favourite flower... such a brave little flower. Daisy's birthday is very soon... Pied

Knuston Hall

wild flowers all along th
red campion
Ox eye daisy
Hemlock

I meant to do my work today –
But a brown bird sang
in the
apple tree...

Richard Galliene...

Charing to Knebworth...

Parsley ragwort, red campion...

...es of the motorway... white campion...

Knebworth to Knuston Hall...

Knuston Hall 30/5/12 – 1/6/12...

Common Comfrey

The leaves will decay to release a large amount of absorb plant nutrien...

Very wet weather – but the wild flowers were very happy!...

Smooth Sowthistle...

...nton to Sylva every da...

Mixing paper and fabric of different types can make your journal far more interesting to complete.

Daily journals can have extra pages sewn in where appropriate. (see spread below) Print, add pressed flowers, recipes from magazines and brochures or family sayings! ...

All materials for this book were bought while staying in France. The book was then made up there.

OCTOBER / NOVEMBER

FRANCE

This book was made from old linen. A very thin coat of watered down Gesso was painted on the fabric and dried, before making up the book.

4th – Devon.

Buckland Abbey to meet Lindsay and Pete. Laughed a lot!

Bee on the new ceiling in plaster.

14th November...   It was supposed to protect the meat from mi...

Butchers were thought to cover their meat with the plant.

butcher's broom

ingle pages an be bonded r glued on...

of the mint family...

...in the woods...

MOROCCAN LAMB TAGINE

Serves 4.

2 lamb shanks
1 medium size onion (finely chopped)
...ves of garlic, ...eeled and roughly ...opped)
...p honey

Grenville arms on the guest house —

window

near front entrance...

Buckland Abbey was also the home of Sir Roger Grenville who went down with 'Mary Rose' in 1545......

MATERIALS

FABRIC

Fabric makes wonderful books especially if you love to stitch. Fabrics like - calico, old cotton sheets, linen, tablecloths, napkins etc and some printed fabrics. Vintage fabrics seem to get softer with age and are lovely to work with. Thinner fabrics will need bonding together and some fabrics will need priming with a thin layer of Gesso before working on them.

PAPER.

All kinds of papers can be used for covers and pages - really it is just trial and error.
I use wallpaper lining paper (1000 grade is ideal) brown paper of various sorts and tissue (Abaca)
The important factors to remember are — the paper has to be robust and flexible enough to stand painting, folding and stitching — you don't want a book that has pages which are too flimsy or stiff.

BONDAWEB/WONDERUNDER

An adhesive web for fabric in sheet form, activated by heat (applied with an iron).

GLUE

For sticking small items into books, a simple glue stick is useful, but PVA is longer lasting. Use PVA also for larger applications.

ABACA TISSUE.

100% Abaca Fibre - great strength even when wet. Can be bonded to felt, calico, cotton sheeting etc for covers and bonded together to make pages.

FUNKY FOAM

Funky foam is a thin dense foam sheet which can be made into excellent printing blocks Draw or trace onto the foam with a pencil, cut out the shape and glue to a piece of mounting board or similar. When the glue is dry further details can be added to the foam block.

Clean blocks with a babywipe, do not immerse in water.

ACRYLIC WAX

Acrylic wax is resistant to heat and water.
It can be applied on any porous surface
making it feel like it is coated with beeswax.
It can be applied with a brush over most
mediums from watercolour to fabric paint pro-
viding a seal, enhancing the colour and
improving the feel of the item. When dry it can
be buffed to a shine. You can also mix colour
and powdered pigments with it. Brushes can be
washed out in warm water.

WATERSOLUBLE INKBLOCKS.

Inkblocks can be used like a crayon - dry, or add
water to create washes. They are permanent
when dry and can be worked on top. Use on
paper or fabric. Also, grate and dissolve in
water and use as a paint.

PENS

There are many pens on the market that are
available for use. I use Artist pens which
come in various widths and colours and
are waterproof and lightfast. Find the pen
that suits you best.

PENCILS

I use a variety of pencils. You can use ordinary coloured pencils to draw with. Watercolour pencils which when used with water can create paintlike effects or inkbased pencils which produce intense colour and washes and are permanent when dissolved. There are many other pencils and crayons which are suitable.

GESSO

Artists' acrylic primer. Used thinly to seal or prime fabric prior to use.
Applied thickly it can be drawn and printed into to create interesting surfaces.

DYE PALETTES

The easiest way to use dye whilst making books is to use a dye based water colour palette such as KOH-I-NOOR. Readily available and easy to use, gives good strong vibrant colours and can be watered down for paler shades when wanted. Works well on fabric and paper.

MY THANKS GO TO

Viv Arthur and Kevin Mead for their love and support.

My family especially my lovely grandaughters Grace and Daisy who love making books with their Nana.

Joe and Zoë Sharratt for their kindness.

Christine and Keith Lockton, Gwen and Mike Rutland, Pauline and John Horne, David and Snowy and Pat Trott for their humour, patience and laughter.

My 'Gang of Four' - Audrey, Charlotte, Christine and Liz.

Not forgetting Stephen Green for his help with the printing of this book.

My darling husband Jim, for his continued creative advice and help and being there for me always.